The Chair Kicked Me and I Kicked it Back

Written by Nina Plonka

Inspired by Kate Plonka

Illustrated by Alfred Herman

The Chair Kicked Me and I
Kicked It Back
Copyright © 2014 by Nina Plonka
All rights reserved.

ISBN-13: 978-1492970927
(CreateSpace-Assigned)

ISBN-10: 1492970921

Prologue

Raising A Child with Sensory Processing Disorder

When Kate was born I would stare at her in amazement and marvel about how perfect she was. However, as she grew I began to notice red flags indicating that she was struggling with something. I wasn't really sure what it was and I hoped she would grow out of it.

When she entered school I knew she would encounter things that would "upset her" but I knew she was strong willed and would find her way.

It was in Kindergarten that her awesome teacher and I realized that we had a real challenge on our hands. There were so many seemingly mundane things that Kate found very difficult and could not deal with, without much anxiety.

Her father and I always hoped that things would be alright. It wasn't until she entered the 2nd grade that it all became clear that we needed more help.

We visited many therapists and doctors and Kate was diagnosed with many things, including OCD and Anxiety disorder and many different medications were prescribed to "help" her.

One therapist suggested I pull Kate out of public school and send her to a special school because of her "difference" and "normal" schools might not be for her. Other professionals tried many ways to understand her inner problems. They used drawings and various games to get out what was troubling her.

In 2013 totally frustrated and confused, I reached out to the SPD (Sensory Processing Disorder) foundation and found the knowledge and support necessary for Kate to begin to reach her potential.

Their understanding, warmth and caring was what we needed. Together, and with the help of so many other people we have learned that there are answers out there. Never give up hope. Above all, let your child know that you love them dearly every day. Please see the end of this book for all the people who helped me get to this point. It does take a village.

To all the other mothers and fathers of kids with SPD (sensory processing disorder) I want to say. NEVER GIVE UP! There are answers out there and people are poised and ready to help. Just seek them out!! Our kids are sensational and it behooves us to let them know that each and every day. Xoxox

Enjoy and learn from Kate's story

Kate...

It was the first day of school and Kate was very excited and very nervous at the same time. She knew there were so many things that were about to happen that would make her feel weird or stressed. So many things that she knew would be hard for her to do, say or feel. On that very first day most kids looked forward to sitting at their very own seat at their very own desk. Kate, however, had other feelings because she suffered from SPD. The very act of sitting with her feet under a desk was terrifying.

She knew that if the teacher "made" her sit close up under the desk she would really get upset and have a "meltdown" as sometimes happens with kids with SPD.

SPD may involve problems with hearing, seeing, smelling, taste, touch, proprioception (understanding where you are in space) and vestibular orientation (balance). They can all misfire and not work right. Sometimes all are involved and sometimes only a few, or only just one.

The signals from Kate's brain did not run smoothly and her body's responses to the signals were not always right. The signals from the brain to her body were like a road full of speed bumps, which made the message difficult to get because the message has to slow down for each speed bump.

For Kate, the sense of touch was sending confusing signals for she hated to sit on hard surfaces and certain clothes were difficult for her to wear. For instance; she hated certain "itchy" fabrics and tags and collars on shirts and some socks and pants were always an issue.

Kate couldn't get too close to other kids or sit too close to the desk or table. It just felt wrong and it upset her and made her feel she was being suffocated.

When the teacher asked Kate to sit at her desk, Kate scowled and said "that chair kicked me and I kicked back and I'm not sitting in it"

It was the first day of school and Kate's reaction puzzled the teacher but she allowed Kate to stand. Kate was relieved but knew the feeling wouldn't last forever and it was just a matter of time before another incident occurred and Kate needed a plan.

At home she talked to her mother and decided to tell her teacher about SPD.

At first the teacher seemed surprised by Kate's outburst but when she thought about it she told Kate she was proud of her for telling her what was wrong and said "I am going to think of something to help you".

The next day the teacher gave Kate something she called her "magical friend".

Beary...

"Beary" was a very soft squishy stuffed bear that could be a friend who would sit with Kate and help her cope with her feelings! She could help Kate redirect what she was feeling into something good; instead of bad. Her teacher told her "You can either sit on her or just hug her and see if that helps."

BEARY

Kate took Beary back to her chair and during quiet time as she was staring at her she began to day dream. Beary's eyes began to move and suddenly she began to speak. She said to Kate "Do you want to come on a journey with me" Kate said "Oh! Yes of course, but where?"

Beary took Kate to her home in "Bears Town" "why don't you tell me what's bothering you and maybe I can help?" Kate thought about it and was too confused and scared to share what she was having a hard time understanding herself but she wanted to try.

Kate thought "I feel like I can trust Beary with what bothers me most". Kate explained to Beary "Sometimes my skin doesn't feel right and when it should feel good it doesn't. Sitting in my chair or having kids close to me scares me". I don't always know why I feel this way but when I do, I can some-times act silly or if it really worries or scares me I can have a "meltdown". "I think the meltdowns scare me the most" she told Beary.

I don't even feel like I am inside my body when they happen. If I can't get away from the situation I feel a warm feeling coming over and I start to sweat and then it seems all my senses go haywire and then I don't remember anything". "It's very scary", Kate explained.

"Kate" Beary said "I know that all of this is so scary to you but I am here with you now and it's going to be alright." She knew that.

"Sensory processing disorder is different for all kids. Some kids don't like to be touched or hugged and others can't get enough they need to be hugged all the time. Some kids don't like to swing on the jungle gym; climb on things and others can't spin and jump enough."

"Kate" said Beary what if I could introduce you to other kids just like you? Would you want to meet them?

"Oh yes!" Kate replied. Beary took Kate to a gigantic room that looked like the cafeteria or gym of an elementary school, as she entered, she was absolutely amazed.

There were kids everywhere: - some reading quietly, some running around in circles and others were climbing on the jungle gym and ropes. Kate asked Beary "What kind of place is this?" Beary smiled It's the how I feel gym!" All the kids in here have some type of SPD. The kids were of all different cultures and backgrounds.

"Let me introduce you to a few people, Kate."

First I would like you to meet Kevin he is 7 and he struggles with auditory processing disorder" said Beary. So Kevin struggles with hearing and recognizing sounds.

"Hi! Kate". "I can get very frustrated in class when I try to answer the teacher's questions and I am just not fast enough to raise my hand and someone else answers before me" said Kevin. "That sounds very frustrating Kevin, nice meeting you" said Kate.

"Oh and over there is Emily she is 12 and has Oral Defensiveness", said Beary. She only eats certain foods and no two foods can touch on the plate. Emily, come on over and meet Kate".

"Hi! Kate, I am very picky with my foods and I only like certain textures and types of food. I also hate brushing my teeth it's very painful for me. But I know I have to do it. My mom still has to watch to make sure I do it", explained Emily. "Wow" Kate said "that sounds like me I don't like to brush my teeth or my hair, but I do love to eat all kinds of foods"

Finally, I want you to meet Jimmy he's 4 and he suffers from proprioceptive dysfunction. "Hi Jimmy", said Beary. Jimmy turned around to say hi and fell over.

"Oh no! Are you ok", said Kate. "Yes I am ok that happens all the time" said Jimmy. "I have a real hard time with balance and coordination.

When I grow up I want to be a baseball player, but I have a lot of work to do still to learn to catch the ball and run like other kids do. Someday I hope to ride a bike too. I can get really angry sometimes because my body doesn't listen to me when I tell it to move."

Beary looked over and Kate had a small tear running down her face, she was so sad for Jimmy. She asked Beary if Jimmy was going to be alright. Beary told her "he's got a long road ahead but he's a tough kid".

Kate listened intently as Beary went on, "You see Kate each person is like a snow flake different in every way" Said Beary.

"All these kids didn't do anything wrong nor did their families, it's just that so many things are happening at the same time, and we need to work on paving the road smoothly instead of all these speed bumps which get stuff caught up."

Beary said "Come on Kate I want to show you a world where there is NO SPD and you can see how all of your lives will look one day.

On a big TV screen Kate saw how happy she would be sitting at school with her collared uniform, running and playing, fitting in with the other kids and she said to Beary "I am so going to beat this SPD and I love you Beary for introducing me to other kids just like "ME".

"I know you will" Beary replied.

"**K**ate are you ready to go back home now? Asked Beary. "I wish I could stay here forever, but I have work to do, so, yes I am ready" answered Kate.

"Good I am going to spin you around 5 times and when I am done I know you will be on your way to dealing with all the SPD challenges ahead".

"Kate, when you get back to class and feel stressed or nervous and need to sit or take a test, sometimes it is easier to sit on a friend's lap, why don't you sit on my lap, don't worry you won't squish me" said Beary.

Kate and Beary chuckled together.

Kate was overjoyed with the idea that she could someday be just like every other kid.

The next thing Kate heard was her teacher calling her "Kate, Kate are you ok?" snapping out of her daydream, Kate answered "Yes, I'm feeling wonderful."

She now realized that things were possible as Beary had shown her.

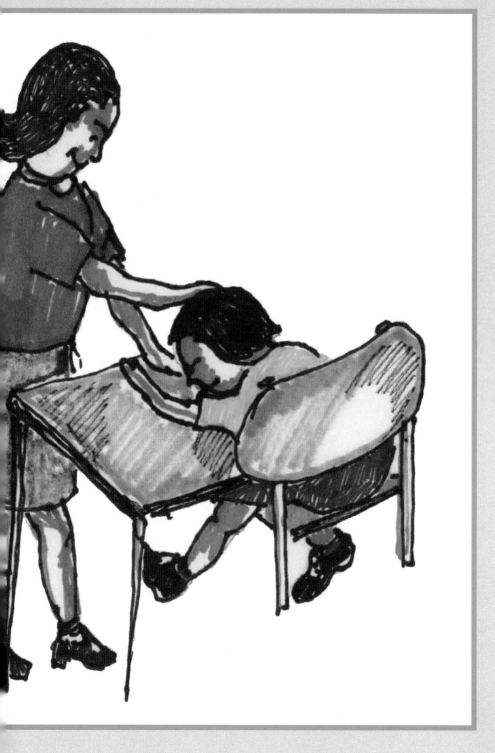

Kate did sit on Beary for the first few weeks and then she simply had Beary next to her. After a while she realized that she "could" sit knowing that Beary was in her backpack.

Kate often thought of the kids she met in "It's How I Feel Gym" and hoped they all would find their road smoother over time.

All the kids in Kate's class learned of Beary and why Kate needed her. Much to Kate's surprise and joy some stood by her and supported her and loved Beary too. Some others didn't and that was a life lesson for Kate.

By the end of school that year Beary simply stayed at home with her other stuffed animals and Kate knew she was always there if she needed her and that she "could" teach her brain to be ok with school and clothes.

Kate learned that sharing something difficult with a trusted adult is good and that the teacher understood and did not judge her. Kate has a long road ahead of her and still is working through her "touch problems" tactile defensiveness and may never "cure her SPD" but she will surely find ways to adapt, knowing that good people are there to help her makes the journey bearable.

Thank you...

I want to thank Rebecca Gonzalez a volunteer mom from SPD for being the first to reach out to me with love and understanding. You are my rock star.

Shannon Visentin (Thera-peds) Kate's OT was the first to let me see the light at the end of the tunnel. Your support and love for Kate plus tons of reading materials let me know that I was doing the right thing.

I need to thank Renee Chillcott from (Center for Brain Training) who helped Kate holistically smooth the road in her brain.

I must thank my wonderful friend Melissa Ringel who was always there for us day or night with non-judgmental love. My rock!

The most important thank you however must go to Steven Plonka, my amazing husband and Kate's dad for being the BEST dad a kid could ask for, Kate always came first. He always believed that WE would figure this out and Kate would shine.

Finally Kate, I love you now and forever. You are the most caring, thoughtful and loving person. The knowledge you have gained for your experience will serve you well in life and I know you will continue to shine. There are kids out there that will learn and know they are NOT alone because you were willing to share your story. You will be an inspiration for all of them.

About the Author

Nina Plonka RN, BSN is a registered nurse working as a Director in home health care in South Florida. But she is a mother first and her love for her daughter inspired her to research, read and asked questions until she figured out what was wrong with her daughter and how to fix it. All along Nina documented the journey to someday be able to help others understand this disorder. It was a long process with many heart breaks and life lessons, but in the end Kate is making great strides and fast approaching Middle school.

Made in the USA
Coppell, TX
26 January 2020